The
SPUR BOOK
of
ORIENTEERING

The
SPUR BOOK
of
ORIENTEERING

Roger Smith

SPURBOOKS LIMITED

Published by
SPURBOOKS LIMITED
6 Parade Court
Bourne End
Buckinghamshire

ISBN 0 904978 99 0

Printed by Maund & Irvine, Ltd., Tring, Herts.

CONTENTS

INTRODUCTION

ABOUT THIS SERIES

Venture Guides are written for those people who enjoy outdoor activities, and they fall into two broad areas.

The first group covers skills and techniques which all outdoor people should possess whatever their particular outdoor interest. The books in this group therefore cover such subjects as Knot Tying and Splicing, Map and Compass work, Outdoor Cooking and Camping skills, First Aid, Weather Lore, and Survival and Rescue techniques.

The second group covers what describe as venture sports, that is, activities which require little mechanical equipment and are not team games. This group contains books on Downhill and Cross-Country Skiing, Rock Climbing, Backpacking, Hilltrekking. Sailing, Canoeing, and now, the subject of this book, Orienteering.

All Venture Guides are written for beginners. A new series, the Spurbook Master Guides, will cover advanced aspects of some of these activities.

ABOUT THIS BOOK

Orienteering is a growing sport combining the fitness of the runner with the skill of the map reader — 'cunning running' is indeed what it is sometimes called.

In this book, Roger Smith, an experienced orienteer, provides all the basic information necessary to make a start with this enjoyable and exciting activity.

FIGURE 1

Chapter 1

WHAT IS ORIENTEERING?

BASIC PRINCIPLES

On being faced with the word 'orienteering', people's reactions vary from thinking it's some new form of martial art from the East, through 'oh yes, we did that in the Army (or scouts)' to blank incomprehension. So what *is* orienteering?

It is a sport, or recreation, which involves the participant (the *orienteer)* in completing a course of any length from one kilometre to 12 kilometres or more, usually in open or wooded country, visiting a number of checkpoints (or *controls* as they are more normally called) en-route. The precise location of each control, with a brief description of it and the code which is to be found on the marker hung at it (the *control flag*) are given to the orienteer at the start of the course. The route he chooses between each control, and the speed at which he travels, are entirely his own choice.

His aids are a compass, a very detailed large-scale map especially drawn for orienteering use, and his wits. These last are most important as the problems of navigation and route choice are the essence of orienteering, and provide much of the sport's unique enjoyment. Skill in route selection and map-reading are just as important as physical fitness, and this vital factor — the involvement of mind as well as body — makes orienteering, in the writer's opinion, about the most complete recreation yet invented by man.

Orienteering events always include courses suitable for all ages and levels of ability and fitness — so don't be afraid that it's something you can't do. If you can walk, you can orienteer. Another great blessing is that competitors are set off individually, not en masse as in cross-country races, so there's no question of being 'left behind' in a mad stampede to reach the first control! Of course this means that, if you do make an error and become temporarily lost, you must work out your own salvation. There are well-tried techniques for doing this, as we shall see in Chapter 6.

After reading this book you should have sufficient knowledge to go out and complete a simple orienteering course. I hope that you will then come back another time, as more and more people are doing.

A GROWING SPORT

Orienteering does not have a long history. It originated in Scandinavia in the 1920s as a way of giving young people healthy exercise using the great available natural resource of forest. Now it is a world sport, practised everywhere from Australia to Finland, from Britain to Japan.

We can effectively date the introduction of orienteering to Britain as 1962, when a group of Swedish orienteers from the Stockholms OK club organised an event on the Duke of Atholl's estate at Dunkeld in Scotland, and gave it the grand name of the *'First Scottish Orienteering Championships'*. Nine Swedes took part, and they filled the first nine places in the results. The other entrants were mostly members of Scottish athletic clubs. They found the new sport interesting enough to want to try it again; further events were organised, and a Scottish Orienteering Association was formed.

Throughout the mid-1960s, pockets of orienteering activity sprang up all over Britain, and in 1965 an English O.A. was formed. As in history, so in orienteering, it was inevitable that English and Scots should get together, and the present national body for the sport, the British Orienteering Federation, was formed in 1968. In the ensuing ten years both the number of events and the numbers taking part have grown steadily, and membership of the B.O.F. stands today at around 10,000. It is not unusual to find 500 competitors at even a local event; championships regularly attract over 1,000, and the Jan Kjellstrom Trophy, an international event held every Easter in a different region of Britain, drew 2,400 orienteers from 10 nations to Sheffield in March 1978.

Don't be put off by these impressive statistics. Once you're out on the course there's little sense of a crowd of people around you. The larger number taking part have meant that more clubs are being formed, making it easier for the newcomer to find a club locally and to make contact with other orienteers. You'll soon get to know people, and one of the nicest parts of any orienteering event is the 'post-mortem' in the car park or event centre afterwards, when everyone swaps tales of joy and misery about their run.

A FAMILY SPORT

At the 1977 British Championships on Cannock Chase, the youngest competitor was 8 and the oldest 72 — not many sports could boast that age range! The spread of courses, with lengths from 2km or less up to 10km or even more, available at events means that orienteering truly is a family sport. While Dad is grappling with the problems of a longer course (perhaps racing his older children), Mum and the younger ones can try a short course — either individually or as a group, whichever they prefer. It's not unusual for it to be the other way round, with the lady being the keen one and Dad content to walk round! Orienteering has a marvellously flexible structure, and has been carefully developed to keep it that way so that it has never become either an 'elitist' sport for superfit athletes only or a purely non-competitive recreation.

A GREAT SPORT FOR JUNIORS

Many children take very naturally to orienteering, seeming to find it more fun and more exciting than organised team games. It is indeed a sport that the 'non-ball types', the duffers at football, cricket or hockey, can enjoy and even win prizes at.

Orienteering is now a recognised sports activity at many schools, and at most universities (in Sweden it is taught as part of the basic cirriculum). It needs, of course, a teacher with the time and dedication to take the children to events, look after them, and bring them back again. Orienteering has traditionally been a Sunday activity (so that it would not clash with other sports) but several regions, such as the East Midlands, are organising Junior Leagues with events on Saturday mornings to ease the transport problem, and these leagues are proving very successful.

The introduction of colour-coded courses and regional badge schemes (see Chapter 3) has given juniors a further incentive to improve their performances. But the very nature of orienteering, which has to take place in fairly inaccessible areas, means that too many children simply drop out of the sport when they leave school. This is a problem we have yet to solve.

Many children also come into orienteering with, or through, their parents (not a few have dragged their protesting parents along in the first place!). If the whole family enjoy the sport, the children will naturally tend to stay with it.

Orienteering teaches children something about the countryside, map-reading and compass work (a very useful skill), can help them with their geography lessons, and perhaps best of all encourages them to be self-sufficient. They get a real sense of achievement in completing an orienteering course.

11

IS IT EXPENSIVE?

The answer to this question is no, not necessarily. You can complete orienteering courses perfectly happily wearing ordinary outdoor walking clothes or a tracksuit and training shoes or boots. You will need a whistle and a mapcase (a few pence each) and a compass (£2-£5) after you have done a few events and get on to harder courses. Entry to local events is about 30-40 pence, often less for juniors under 19. You also need a red biro or wax pencil to mark the course on to your map. There *is* specialist gear, of course, as there is with any sport, and this is discussed in Chapter 4. But you won't need it to begin with, and may not need it at all.

The main cost involved in orienteering is undoubtedly that of getting to and from events. If you are content with local competitions this may not amount to much. But if, like most orienteers, you want to widen your area to experience and enjoy different types of terrain, the cost of getting there and back again mounts up. This cost is far outweighed, however, by the pleasure you will get from the sport and the friends you will make.

WAYFINDING

Without trying to confuse you, it must be said at the beginning that orienteering is really two activities in one. There is the really competitive side of the sport, where seconds count and you try your hardest to get round the course as quickly as you can. And there is the less- or non-competitive side, often practised by families, where it is treated as a pleasant Sunday recreation, completion of the course is sufficient achievement in itself, and speed of progress is not important. This sort of orienteering tends to be called 'Wayfinding' or 'Wayfaring' and you will often find 'Wayfinding Courses' offered at orienteering events.

I explain this merely so that you will not be confused by the appearance of the word 'Wayfinding' in event details when you start orienteering. Wayfinders use the same map and terrain as all other orienteers, though they tend to be given separate courses to save them being trampled underfoot by hulking young men travelling at high speed. They are welcome members of the orienteering community and are in no way regarded as inferior to their championship-chasing cousins.

Chapter 2

THE ORIENTEERING MAP

"A map is a window to adventure" wrote the late Sir Francis Chichester. He was the B.O.F.'s first President, and gave us the 'Chichester Trophy' which is awarded each year for the best contribution to mapping. If I may paraphrase the great man slightly, an orienteering map might be described as "a picture of adventure": adventure yet to come, and adventure that has been.

Why is a special map necessary? Basically because the nature of orienteering with its emphasis on fine navigation, demands a map showing much more small detail than most maps have room for. Many readers will be familiar with the Ordnance Survey 1:50000 maps. These are very fine maps indeed, but their scale is too small for orienteering. If you look at a piece of woodland on the OS map, you will see that the main topographical features are shown — the contours, the streams, and so on. Orienteering demands much more information so that courses can be set which bring all the skills of the game into play, and so that those attempting those courses have as full a picture of the ground as is possible. Orienteering maps are therefore specially surveyed and drawn at large scales — 1:15000, 1:10000, or even larger if very small and detailed areas are being used.

FINDING AN AREA

All over the country, orienteering clubs are pouring over OS maps (see how useful they are!) picking out the 'green bits' and then going out to look at them to see if they are suitable for orienteering. Ideally, the wood should be mature, with a clean floor and well-spaced trees: when you get these conditions, as in parts of the New Forest or on Cannock Chase, orienteering is a delight. However, more often the wood will be open in some places, thick in others; there will be patches of dense undergrowth, tangled fallen trees, or other obstructions. So most areas are a compromise. But with detailed mapping and skilful course planning, excellent events can be staged in what at first sight appear rather unpromising areas — so don't be disheartened!

Assuming that the club has found a suitable area, and obtained the landowner's permission to map it and put on an event, the next stage is the survey.

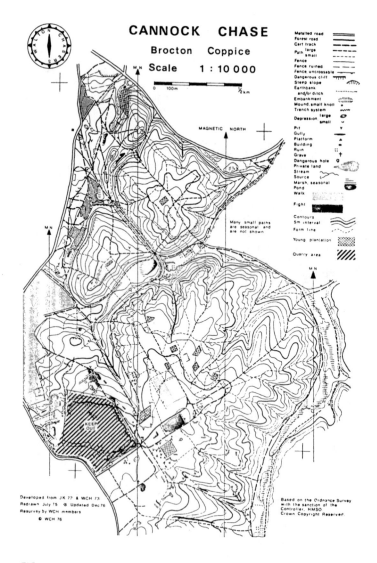

CANNOCK CHASE

Brocton Coppice

Scale 1 : 10 000

Metalled road	
Forest road	
Cart track	
Path large	
small	
Fence	
Fence ruined	
Fence uncrossable	
Dangerous cliff	
Steep slope	
Earthbank and/or ditch	
Embankment	
Mound, small knoll	
Trench system	
Depression large	
small	
Pit	
Gully	
Platform	
Building	
Ruin	
Grave	
Dangerous hole	
Private land	
Stream	
Source	
Marsh, seasonal	
Pond	
Walk	
Fight	
Contours 5m interval	
Form line	
Young plantation	
Quarry area	

Many small paths are seasonal and are not shown

Developed from JK 72 & WCH 73
Redrawn July 75   Updated Dec 76
Resurvey by WCH members
© WCH 76

Based on the Ordnance Survey with the sanction of the Controller, HMSO Crown Copyright Reserved

FIGURE 2

14

THE SURVEY

Orienteering maps may be surveyed by one person, a small group, or a larger team working under an overall leader. First of all, the major linear features such as roads, tracks, walls, and streams will be drawn on to a base map — often at twice the scale of the finished map. The area is then generally divided up into small 'parcels' with sides about 400 metres long, and each parcel is surveyed in detail to locate and plot any features which could be used as control sites, and any other information which the competitor will need to know, such as the denseness of vegetation.

This surveying may well take many months of weekend work. When it is all completed, the person who is actually going to draw the map collates all the information from the survey on to a master copy of the base map, ready for drawing up.

Areas which are going to be used for major events such as Championships are often surveyed a year before the event so that the area is seen in the same condition as it will be in when the event is held.

DRAWING AND PRINTING

The map is drawn on sheets of transparent film using special fine drawing pens of the 'Rotring' type, with different nib thicknesses used to show different features (e.g. major tracks are drawn thicker than small paths). Shading and tone indicates the type of vegetation and the 'runnability' (of which more later).

Orienteering maps are commonly printed in three or four colours and the sheet for each colour has to be drawn separately. The overall 'register' (the relative accuracy of each colour to all the other colours) is maintained by fastening the sheets together when drawing. In addition, 'register marks' are placed on each sheet, and you should always check your map when you get it at an event to see that the register is good — the crosses should coincide exactly. If they don't, the register is inaccurate and this can lead to the map giving you misleading informtion. For instance, if the blue and black registers are out of coincidence, a ditch or stream could appear on the wrong side of a path. This rarely happens, but it is always worth a check.

There are now a number of printers who specialise in printing orienteering maps. You can be sure that a modern orienteering map is an accurate and carefully-produced representation of the terrain it covers. Many of them are almost works of art — and never forget that the people producing them are amateur cartographers. Mapping can become so absorbing as a pastime that there are some orienteers who prefer it to competing. Maybe you'll help to make a map yourself one day.

A PICTURE OF THE GROUND

The experienced orienteer relates map to terrain and vice versa almost instantaneously, relying on the mapper to provide him with an accurate picture of the ground he is running over. When you start orienteering, you will not, of course, be blessed with this skill, but you start to develop it from the moment you set out on your first orienteering course, map in hand. The mapper has gone to great lengths to provide you with all the information you are likely to need in order to complete the course and to make your route choice as wide and as fair as possible. To begin with, you will be mainly concerned with larger features such as tracks, walls and streams, but gradually you will learn to 'fill in' the picture, noting all the information provided by the map and using it to best advantage. This skill is covered in more detail in Chapter 6.

HOW THE MAP HELPS

Don't be afraid of an orienteering map: it may look very complicated, with its different colours, shadings, and symbols, but you'll quickly come to see it as a friend. It shows you the shape of the land you're crossing, the good and not-so-good areas for running or walking, and all the features, large and small, that you'll pass on your way round the course. To navigate across an area of open forest, checking off features as you pass them, and then 'home in' on the control maker at the end is a great feeling. It happens surprisingly often, too! In the early days of orienteering, maps were just photocopies of the Ordnance Survey map (often at 1:25000) or rather crude attempts at redrawing in one or two colours. The newcomer to orienteering nowadays is fortunate in that mapping has developed to a very high level of skill. So put your trust in the map — and if the terrain seems not to agree with the map, it's almost certainly you in the wrong place rather than the mapper being inaccurate.

THE SYMBOLS EXPLAINED

The main symbols used on orienteering maps in Britain are shown below, colour by colour, with a brief explanation of the feature described by each symbol.

MAP SYMBOLS

Black

═══════════	Metalled road.
▬▬▬▬▬▬▬	Unmetalled or forest road.
▬ ▬ ▬ ▬ ▬ ▪	Track (may be driveable).
▫ ▫ ▫ ▫ ▫ ▫	Broad footpath.
⋯⋯⋯⋯⋯⋯	Narrow footpath.
▬ ▬ ▬ ▬ ▬	Ride or firebreak. This is a gap between trees to help forest working or check fire. It may be very wide, but the surface is often rough.
•+•+•+•+•+•	Wall (stone).
▬▬▬▬▬▬	Fence.
	n.b. the above two symbols, when shown as a broken line, indicate a ruined wall or fence. Hedges are not usually shown.
⋯⋯⋯⋯⋯	Vegetation change. If this is shown on the map, the change must be clear to the eye, e.g. a change from deciduous to coniferous trees, or from forest to moorland.
▬▬▬z▬▬	Power line.
▬▬▬▬▬▬	Dangerous cliff (go round these, not up or down them).
⊓⊓⊓⊓⊓⊓	Small cliff or crag (not an obstacle).
•	Boulder — i.e. a significant single stone.
⁂	Boulder field — to be avoided.
■	Building.
⊏ ⊐	Ruin. This may be crumbling walls or merely a foundation, but the shape must be discernible on the ground.
⌐⌐⌐⌐⌐	Felled area (overprinted on yellow open ground symbol). These areas have often been recently felled and may be difficult to cross. Cairn or boundary stone.

Brown

Contour (each fourth contour may be thicker. The downhill side of contours is often indicated by a tick).

Form line. This is used to indicate a small ground feature between two contour lines.

Re-entrant. This is the term used in orienteering to denote a valley or large gully. Often there is a stream in the bottom.

Spur. The exact opposite of a re-entrant — a 'nose' of land projecting between two valleys.

$\in \ni$ Large depression or pit.

U OR V Small depression.

-( )- Large knoll or hill summit.

• Small knoll or hilltop.

················ Earthbank. There are many of these in British woods — often they show the course of old field boundaries.

▲ Platform. Nothing to do with trains — it is a small projection from a hill slope, too small to be marked as a spur.

━━━ Gully (or dry ditch).

ππππππππππ Steep earth bank with no rock visible.

Blue

⬭ Pond or lake, edge defined in black.

━━━ River, edges defined in black. Usually crossable only at a bridge or ford.

━━━ Stream. Usually crossable.

– – – – – Ditch — may be dry in summer and autumn.

≣≣≣ Marshy ground.

←━━ Spring or stream source.

o Well.

□ Water tank.

∪ Waterhole.

⌀ Small pond.

Note: on many maps, the magnetic north lines are drawn in blue to avoid any confusion with paths or power lines. Don't look for the north-south stream if it is a north line.

18

Yellow

Solid yellow indicates open land — usually grassland. A yellow dot or line screen indicates rough open land such as moorland if it has black mixed with it, or land with scattered tress if without.

Green

Green screening is used on orienteering maps to indicate the vegetation density, and thus the 'runnability' of the area. A simple rough guide is that the darker the green, the slower the going. Solid green is known with reason as 'fight' and should be avoided unless you enjoy pushing through close-packed spruce trees! Where no shading is shown, the area should be runnable, with little or no obstruction to progress.

Chapter 3

WHICH COURSE?

One of the most common complaints made by newcomers to orienteering is that they find the number of courses offered at events, and all the different age-groups, rather bewildering. This chapter sets out to explain the options available and to show the beginner how to make a logical progression 'up the scale'.

KNOW YOUR LIMITS

Most orienteering events offer at least four courses of varying length and difficulty. Large events have more, and championships, where each age-class has a separate course, may have 20 courses.

The new orienteer is well advised to start with the shortest course available. This will probably be about 2km in length, and will be simple to complete, with few navigational problems. If this is not enough, it is usually possible to try another, slightly longer course, often at no extra charge.

As in life, so in orienteering, you must learn to walk before you can run. It's no good charging off into the woods at high speed if you've no idea what you're heading for. You will end up a minute later rather lost, and completely out of touch with the map. Start by walking round short courses, getting used to the scale of the maps, symbols, using your compass, and practising simple navigational techniques as outlined in Chapter 6. When you are happy that you can get round without problems, try the next course up in length.

THE BOF AGE-GROUPS

One of the pleasures of orienteering is that it frequently offers you a new challenge by moving you into another age-group. The classes adopted in competition in Britain are:

Class	Age
M10, W10	10 and under
M11, W11	11-12
M13, W13	13-14
M15, W15	15-16
M17, W17	17-18
M19	19-20
M21	21-34
W19	19-34

M35, W35	35-42
M43, W43	43-49
M50, W50	50-55
M56, W56	56 and over

M stands for men (and boys) and W for women (and girls).

You will see that a very wide range of ages is catered for — those at either end of the scale are among the keenest competitors! There is no 'W21' class, the ladies going from W19 to W35.

The class you compete in is determined by the age you reach during the year — everyone born in 1961 is thus M17 or W17 for the whole of 1978, regardless of whether their birthday is in January or December. This can lead to the odd anomaly like the author recording his only championship win in M35 two months *before* his 35th birthday!

Course lengths start very short (2km or so) for M/W10, gradually get longer up to M21 (10km or more) and W19 (7-8km) and then decrease to 3-4km for M/W56. Men's courses are longer than women's of the same age-group, but not necessarily more difficult. We expect the girls to navigate just as well as the boys, even if they can't run quite as fast or as far. There is nothing to stop anyone doing a course *below* their true age group, and beginners are encouraged to do so, but you should not run in a class *above* your own (e.g. an M17 can run the M15 course but not M19, and M35 can run M43 but not M21).

COLOUR-CODED COURSES

Having got age-groups sorted out, it may seem strange to introduce an entirely different system. Many regions of BOF, however, are now finding that is is preferable to grade courses by their length and difficulty rather than recommending certain courses for certain age-groups. This is called 'colour-coding': it seems to work very well, and gives newcomers a very logical progession that they easily understand.

At events using this system, instead of the shortest and easiest course being labelled say 'M10/W10/W11/W56' it is simply called 'White' and *anyone* can enter it, regardless of age or sex. Beginners are always advised to start on White courses, which are very simple and are designed to give confidence to the newcomer. The next course is Yellow, and the colours gradually became stronger as the courses go up in length and difficulty. The full range is:

Colour	Type of Course	Average Lgth
White	Very short and easy	2km
Yellow	Longer but still easy	3km
Orange	A little more difficult	4km
Green	Same length as Orange but harder	4km
Blue	Longer and harder	5-6km
Red	For the experienced only	7km+

These courses are often used for regional 'Badge schemes' in which a certificate is awarded for successful completion of three courses of any colour except White within a 'par' time. The advantage of this scheme over the BOF National Badge Scheme (see below) is that the 'par' time is declared *before* the event, and is thus not affected by anyone having a 'flyer' and setting very high standards for badge calculations.

Personally, I feel colour-coded courses have much to recommend them: they make life simpler for competitors and organisers, and I would like to see them used nationally.

THE NATIONAL BADGE SCHEME

The National Badge Scheme run by BOF is designed to act as an incentive for competitive orienteers to improve their personal performance, and to maintain it at a high standard once that level is reached.

Badges are awarded at four levels — Gold, Silver, Bronze and Iron, for all age-groups in both sexes. To gain a badge, you must complete three courses at designated qualifying events, called 'Badge Events', with a certain time, related to the leaders in your class. The standards used are:

Gold — The average of the first 3 in the class plus 25%
Silver —   "   "   "   "   plus 50%
Bronze —   "   "   "   "   plus 100%
Iron — Successful completion of the course

You must achieve your three times within a period of two calendar years, and the standard thus achieved remains current for two years also. It is generally recommended that juniors should achieve Gold standard in their own age-group before attempting Badge courses of a higher group.

As an example of how Badge qualifying times are worked out, let us say you ran in a Badge event in the M17 class and the first three in the class recorded 59.30, 60.00, and 60.30. The average of these times is 60 minutes exactly, the qualifying times for M17 badges at that event would be 60 + 25% = 75 minutes for Gold, 60 + 50% = 90 minutes for Silver, and 60 + 100% = 120 minutes for Bronze. Naturally it is rarely that simple, and many are the furrowed brows as event organisers try to work out Badge qualifying times.

Badge events, badges awarded, and details of how to claim your badge are regularly listed in *The Orienteer.*

WAYFINDING AND NON-COMPETITIVE COURSES

Orienteering competitions are run 'against the clock' — competitors in each class are started at one or two-minute intervals and the winner is the person who completes the course in the fastest time. When you start orienteering, you will not really be interested in times — just completing the course will be satisfaction enough.

Orienteering is many things to many people. You may decide that you want to treat it as a competitive sport, and will quickly start to compare your times with others on the same course. You may, on the other hand, treat it just as a pleasant recreation, and remain largely unconcerned with times and placings.

At events using colour-coded courses, it doesn't really matter whether you're fiercely competitive or not bothered with speed at all — you just do whichever course you're happy with. At Badge and other events using the BOF age-classes, however those not wishing to be timed are called 'Wayfinders' and have their own courses. As explained in Chapter 1, these courses often have their own start and finish and their own controls. Wayfinders are usually times only to the nearest minute, but their times appear in the event results the same as all those on the competitive courses.

COMPETING IN PAIRS OR GROUPS

There is nothing to stop newcomers, juniors, or families going round a course in pairs or groups. Many families go on doing this even when they are quite experienced, and juniors are encouraged to go in twos until they have the confidence to compete on their own.

Orienteering moves the old adage up by one — 'Three's company, four's a crowd'. Groups of more than three are not generally encouraged, for fairly obvious reasons. With four or more, at least one of the group hardly gets a look at the map, and they do tend to attract others to controls by their presence.

Pairs and groups cannot qualify for badges under the National Badge Scheme.

Chapter 4

CLOTHING AND EQUIPMENT

Like all sports, orienteering has its range of specialised clothing and footwear. These are not necessary for the beginner, and the alternatives — as well as the special gear — are discussed in this chapter.

FOOTWEAR

It would be generally accepted, I think, that one can tolerate a wet body more easily than wet feet, and as orienteering takes place in open, and often quite rough, country, good protection against bad conditions underfoot is a must for the beginner.

For your first few events, stout shoes suitable for walking in the country will be fine. Walking boots are better as they give some degree of ankle protection, which may help as the ground under your feet will rarely be level or consistent in surface. Training shoes are also adequate for most beginners events. It might be wise to take a choice of footwear and ask at the event about the terrain. If it's dry and firm underfoot, trainers or shoes should be ok., but if its a wettish area with lots of streams, mud and marsh, you will be happier with the added protection of a boot. 'Wellies' are favoured by many wayfinders and as long as you're not in too much of a hurry they will keep your feet quite dry and comfortable.

If you *do* intend to run, you might consider the purchase of a pair of special orienteering shoes worthwhile. These shoes were developed in Scandinavia and have a water-resistant plastic or rubber upper with a multi-studded or barred sole which gives excellent grip on almost any surface except wet rock. They are very light and are cut low on the foot, and are surprisingly hard-wearing — a pair should last even the most dedicated orienteer a couple of seasons. Various makes, including Compass Rose (Swedish), Nokia (Finnish) and Reebok (English) are available from the suppliers listed at the end of the book. You will often find 'mobile shops' operating from a car or van at events. Have a chat to the chap sellng the gear and get him to show you the range of shoes before you make up your mind which ones to buy. Prices are currently (mid-1978) between £7 and £12 per pair.

Whatever shoes you wear, do make sure that your *laces* are in good condition every time you prepare for an orienteering event. And if your shoes or boots get wet, dry them carefully at home,

FIGURE 3

away from direct heat. Orienteering shoes can be washed under a cold tap without harming them, once you have cleaned the mud off. They can then be left to dry (but not near a fire), stuffed with newspaper, until you need them again. Boots should be polished with dubbin or waterproof polish such as *Wet-Pruf.* Orienteering shoes need no polish (I suspect that's why many people buy them).

BODY CLOTHING

Special clothing is certainly not necessary for beginners or wayfinders. A waterproof jacket or anorak with a zip (to adjust the ventilation), light or heavy according to season and corduroy or other strong trousers will be fine. Jeans are *not* recommended as they offer little protection from the elements. A tracksuit, if you have one, is excellent orienteering wear to begin with. Adjust your under-jacket clothing, adding T-shirt or sweater to your shirt, to suit the temperature, remembering that if you're going to be moving fairly slowly and stopping to check the map a lot you're more likely to be cool than hot.

A cap or hat is a good idea if the weather is at all cold or wet. Some 20% or more of body heat-loss is through the head, and if you're warm and dry top and toe, you'll not worry overmuch about the bits in between getting damp.

THE ORIENTEERING SUIT

Like the shoes, the specialist orienteering suit comes from Scandinavia. It is made of a very lightweight 'breathing' nylon, and gives a surprising degree of protection against wind and weather. It's not waterproof, of course, but it will dry on you if you run through a shower and into dry weather again. Its main advantage is its very light weight, giving complete mobility without restricton whilst affording full body cover (of which more in a moment). An alternative favoured by some orienteers (including the author) is knee-length breeches and long socks. The latter are available with a rubberised front panel to minimise scratches when crashing through the undergrowth (the famous 'bramble-bashers'). Light gaiters for the same purpose can also be obtained, and all these items are sold by the same people who supply the shoes. Suits are currently about £8-£10, socks and gaiters about £2.

FIGURE 4

WHY FULL BODY COVER?

It is an inflexible rule in orienteering that body, arms and legs must be fully covered. It might seem silly to have to wear long trousers on a hot summer day, but there is a very good reason for this rule.

In the mid-1960s in Sweden, a large number of orienteers contracted hepatitis (infectious jaundice). They had all been scratched by brambles or undergrowth, and they had all been wearing short-sleeved shirts and/or shorts. The infection was found to have been passed on through sharing washing facilities after events. The 'full body cover' rule was introduced as a counter-measure, to try to eliminate the scratches, and the epidemic disappeared as rapidly as it had arisen. This rule is now operated in all orienteering nations which are members of the International Orienteering Federation, including Britain. It is a sensible precaution and causes no hardship to the competitor. So please respect the rule and don't turn up at the start with bare arms or legs, however warm the day. You will only be asked to go back and cover yourself!

FIGURE 5

MAPCASE, WHISTLE AND PEN

Another safety rule in Britain (though not in some other countries) is that all competitors must carry a whistle. The whistle should only be used if you are completely lost and cannot see any salvation (or any other orienteers), or if you fall and injure yourself (fortunately an extremely rare occurrence). In these cases the signal is six blasts on the whistle at regular intervals of about half a minute. Carrying the whistle presents no problems. It goes into a pocket or on a string round your neck. Very light plastic whistles can be bought for about 12 pence or hired at most events, so don't go and buy an expensive referee-type metal whistle if you haven't got one.

You will also need a pen or pencil to mark down your course, and a mapcase of some kind to keep your map dry and protect it from both the elements and the undergrowth. An ordinary red ball-point pen is quite adequate as a marker, red being the preferred colour for making the course as it does not clash with any of the colours used on orienteering maps. A wax pencil such as a *Chinagraph* is just as good and has the added advantage of making a water-resistant mark.

Special orienteering mapcases are available which have two compartments — a large one for the map and a smaller one for the control card. Both these items must be protected — the map for obvious reasons and the control card as it is your record of having visited all the controls in the correct order, and must be handed in at the finish in reasonable condition so that your time can be recorded on it (your name, class, etc, must also obviously be legible). Any plastic bag thin enough to see through will serve as a mapcase to begin with, but the special orienteering mapcase is so inexpensive and so much better that I advise anyone starting orienteering to acquire a supply as soon as possible. They will save you a lot of trouble.

USING TRANSPASEAL

Another method of protecting your map is to cover it, before you start, with a laminated film of the type used to cover books. The best of these for orienteering purposes is *Matt Transpaseal,* as marks made on it with a Chinagraph-type pencil will not easily rub off, even when wet.

Sheets of Transpaseal can be bought at large stationers or from the ubiquitous gear suppliers at events. The map should preferably be covered back and front, so you need a piece of film slightly more than twice the size of the map (cut to shape if necessary). Peel off the covering paper from half the sheet and place the map carefully on it face up, smoothing out any wrinkles. The back of the map is now protected and you have two alternative ways of covering the front. You can either carry on and do it now, using a chinagraph pencil to mark your course, or (the more advanced method) you can leave the map half done until you reach the master maps, copy down your course in pen in the normal way, and then cover the front of the map. You have to carry with you or dispose of somehow the backing sheet, of course. Whichever of these methods you use, you should end up with a fully-protected map with the course marked pretty well indelibly on it.

THE COMPASS

The protractor-type compass as marketed by Silva and Suunto is the only type practicable for orienteering. It is a marvellous precision instrument, robust in manufacture and simple to use.

The compass and its techniques are described fully in Chapter 8. If you intend to go orienteering regularly you will certainly need a compass. It is a good investment, as you can use it whilst out walking, on holiday, etc. and given reasonable care it should last for years.

HOW TO ARRANGE ALL THE PIECES

You have to carry round the course with you a map, control card, control description sheet, pen, whistle, and compass. The pen (after you've copied your course down with it) and whistle go in a pocket, preferably one with a flap or zip closure (the orienteering suit chest pocket, which is closed by a strip of Velcro, is commonly used). The compass can be tied to your wrist, and a loop of cord is provided with most compasses for just that purpose. Most people keep their compasses either in the hand or ready for instant use, so that really ties up one hand, leaving the other to manage map, control card, and description sheet.

These should obviously, therefore, be made into one unit. How can we do this? A straighforward way is to make full use of an orienteering mapcase. The control card goes in the bottom section, which is cut and shaped to take it. The map goes in the larger section, folded to fit if necessary. One problem with a standard size mapcase is that maps are very far from being a standard size! It is usually possible to fold or trim the map to fit the mapcase without too much difficulty, so that your course is easily visible.

That leaves the control description sheet. It can either be taped on to the back of the map, using transparent adhesive tape or something similar at top *and* bottom for safety, or on the back of the control card, similarly secured. If there is room, and the sheet is small enough, it can be taped on the *front* of the map, which is even better. Either way the control codes and descriptions will be readily available.

It takes only a short time to prepare this 'map unit' after registering and before starting your course, and you will go to the start with everything neatly arranged and ready to hand.

If you are using a plastic bag instead of a proper mapcase, tape the control card to the front of the map at the bottom so that it can't be lost and you can punch the boxes through the bag.

As an alternative, if you are going round as a pair or group, one person can have the responsibility of looking after the control card and making sure it is punched at each control (a good job for a junior orienteer).

A useful tip, regardless of which method you use, is to copy the control codes into the appropriate boxes on the control card (see diagram). Even if you lose your description sheet, you will know the code on the control you are looking for, and if your circles are accurate, the feature should also be apparent.

FIGURE 6

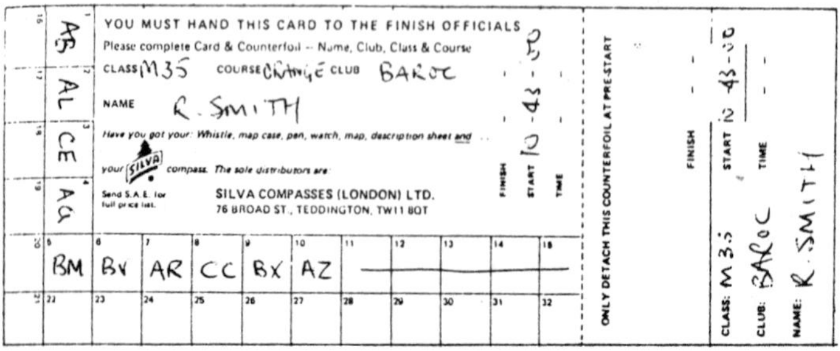

30

Chapter 5

YOUR FIRST EVENT

FINDING OUT ABOUT EVENTS

Orienteering events take place on Sundays almost throughout the year, with a short break in the summer when the undergrowth gets too high in most areas. As has been mentioned, some regions run events on Saturday mornings, but Sunday is the normal orienteering day. How can you find out when and where events will be held in your area? There are several ways of getting this information. The easiest is probably to write to the British Orienteering Federation (Lea Green Sports Centre, Matlock, Derbyshire DE4 5GJ). They will send you details of orienteering in your area, and will also pass your enquiry on to the local club for them to follow up. Or you could ask at your local library for the name and address of the Secretary of the nearest Orienteering club; or, if you have a branch office of the Sports Council in your area, they too should be able to help.

SENDING FOR DETAILS

Let's assume you have found out that John Brown of the local orienteering club is organising a beginners event at Dogwood Common, which is quite near your home, in three weeks time. You decide to go. You *could* just turn up at the common on the day, but it might take you a while to discover the car park and assembly areas, and it is much easier — and more interesting — to send for details. Simply write to Mr. Brown, asking for details of the event and enclosing a stamped addressed envelope *(always send an sae when writing for entry details or other information — it saves the organiser trouble and ensures that you get a rapid reply)*. A few days later your envelope comes back, and you open it to see what's inside.

You will find a sheet giving all the details you need to know about the event, along the lines of the example shown overleaf. Details given include this date and location of the event, where the car park is, when the start times are, how many courses and of what length, and so on. Read these details carefully. In this case, the event is specially designed for newcomers to orienteering, the courses are short and straightforward, and instruction is available should you need it.

At this event, as at most orienteering events, there is no need to enter in advance. This makes life simpler for you; if the weather on the day is awful you can decide to wait for the next event, and you won't have lost any entry fees.

BARCHESTER ORIENTEERING CLUB
invite you to Come and Try Orienteering at

DOGWOOD COMMON
on Sunday, September 24th 1978

Venue: Main car park on B3112. Watch for red and white orienteering signs from the junction with the A35, 4 miles north of Barchester.

Time: Start times from 10.30 a.m. to 1.00 p.m.

Courses: There are four courses available:
White—1.5km—suitable for complete beginners.
Yellow—2.5km—for those with a little experience.
Orange—3.5km—for those with some experince.
Green—5.2km—training course for experienced orienteers only.

Beginners successfully completing the White course may try the Yellow course at no extra charge.

Fee: **19 and over 30p, under 19 15p.**

Map: Scale 1:15,000, redrawn 1978 in 3 colours.

Terrain: Mixed woods and heathland, generally easy going. Very few water features.

Equipment: **Beginners should bring outdoor clothes or tracksuit, stout footwear, red biro, plastic bag for use as mapcase. Compasses and whistles may be hired at the event.**

Facilities: Orange juice at finish. Public toilets and cafe in the car park.

Notes: Experienced orienteers will be on hand to give help and advice to beginners. If it is your first event, please go to the car marked 'beginners' when you arrive.

Organiser: John Brown, 53 North Street, Barchester (tel: 22168) to whom all enquiries should be made.

BEFORE YOU SET OFF
Let's assume, however, that when you get up on the appointed day, the sun is shining (as it does surprisingly often on Sundays)

and you can't wait to get to the event. Hold on a minute. You need to check first that you have everything you need. For your first event, this won't be very much, but it's worth getting into the habit now of making a list the night before and checking before you leave for the event that you have:

Change of clothes
Red pen or wax pencil
Map case (a clear plastic bag will do)
Whistle (can be hired or bought at the event)
Compass–although for a first event you probably won't need one
Lunch and a warm drink
The event details

If you're going round in two pairs, or as individuals, you will need pen, mapcase, and whistle for each. Check, too, that you have all the clothes you need to go round the course and that the laces on the shoes you are going to use are in good condition. The author once lost a race through having a lace break.

ARRIVE IN GOOD TIME
If the event starts at 10.30 a.m. (as many do), arrange your time of leaving the house so that you get there between 10.00 and 10.15. This should enable you to get into the car park easily and will give you time to get everything sorted out without having to rush. It will also give you a chance to sample the 'atmosphere' that is at present even the smallest orienteering event.

When you have reached the venue and parked as directed, take a look around. There will probably be helpful notices about the event, the courses available, the local club, and orienteering in general. A number of cars will be drawn up together with notices on them saying 'Registration' and 'Enquiries'. The people in the enquiries car (or it may be a tent) will be able to tell you anything you want to know about the event, courses, map and so on.

REGISTRATION
When you have decided which course you are going to try, go to the 'Registration' car for that course. Probably you will start with the shortest course (the White course at colour-coded events) so you go to the car marked 'White course' or 'Beginners'.

The procedure here is quite straightforward. The registrar will ask you when you would like to start. If the time is 10.30 when you are registering, give yourself half an hour or so to get ready,

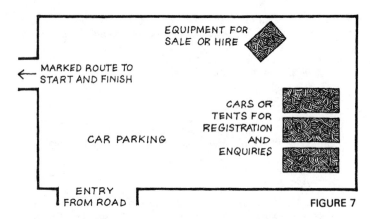

EQUIPMENT FOR
SALE OR HIRE

← MARKED ROUTE TO
START AND FINISH

CARS OR
TENTS FOR
REGISTRATION
AND
ENQUIRIES

CAR PARKING

ENTRY
FROM ROAD

FIGURE 7

and ask for a start time at about 11.00. This assumes that the start is near the car park. Sometimes it isn't — now is the time to find this out, and add a bit to your 'get ready' time if there's a walk of more than a few minutes to the start.

Hand over your entry fee, and in return you will get three or four pieces of paper:

A copy of the *map*
A *control card*
A *control description sheet*
and possibly a sheet giving further information about the course, map, and area.

Take all these back to the car and sort them out as explained in the previous chapter. Before you leave the registration car, it might be as well to fill in a *results envelope*. A box of envelopes is normally provided — fill in your name and address on one, put it back in the box with postage money if requested, and a week or so after the event you will receive a full list of results.

Now let's consider these pieces of paper you have acquired at registration in more detail.

(1) The Map

As explained in Chapter 2, orienteering maps are specially surveyed and drawn for the sport. They show the area in great detail and are at a fairly large scale (often 1:15000 — more than three times the scale of the most-used Ordnance Survey maps). You can rely on these maps to be accurate and helpful. Before you start, have a good look at the map you are going to use. Check the scale. Check the list of symbols, and see if you can find an example of each one on the map. Can you locate the car park? — that will help you to orientate yourself. Is the area flat or hilly (few or many contour lines?), is the wood open or thick (all white or lots of green shading?), are there many tracks, streams, and walls? — and so on. This will only take a few minutes but it is time well spent.

CONTROL CARD

The control card is in two sections. Your start time will already have been filled in at registration. You should now fill in your name(s), club (if you have one — don't worry if you haven't), and class (either use the BOF age-group or just put 'Wayfinders'). Do this on *both sections of the card.* This is important. When you get to the start, you will hand the smaller section (usually called the stub) to one of the officials. Stubs are all carefully filed in start order, and when you finish, the main part of your card will be married up with the stub, so that the organisers know that you are back safely. This simple method of checking ensures that no-one is left out on the course at the end of the event. Accidents can happen, though they are fortunately very rare. The golden rule in orienteering is therefore: ALWAYS REPORT TO THE FINISH, EVEN IF YOU DO NOT COMPLETE THE COURSE. This saves the organisers arranging a search for someone who they think is out in the woods but who is in fact at home with his feet up watching TV!

FIGURE 8

CONTROL DESCRIPTION SHEET

As might be expected from the name, the CDS lists all the controls on your course, the code you will find on each control marker when you reach it (your means of checking that you are at the right control) and gives a brief description of the feature at which the control is hung. A sample CDS might look like this:

White Course — 2.1 km, 6 controls

No	Code	Description
1	AB	Path Junction
2	AC	Path/Stream Crossing
3	AD	Fence Corner
4	AE	Hut, SE Corner
5	AF	Pond, West Side
6	AG	Path Bend

Follow tapes 100 metres to Finish

This shows you that the first control on your course is a path junction, and the control has the code AB on it. When you reach control AB you will know that it is your control, and you will punch your card in the first square to show that you have visited the control. Then you will go on to control AC, the path/stream crossing, and so on round the course, using the CDS as a guide, until you reach control AG, Path Bend, and the magic words 'follow tapes to Finish'. That's a great feeling!

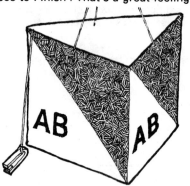

FIGURE 9

MAP CORRECTIONS

At some events, there will be a table or flat area labelled 'map corrections'. Having said repeatedly that orienteering maps are accurate in every detail, it may seem odd to start correcting them. However, if the map was drawn a couple of years ago, and the area is regularly worked (as most British woods are) fences may have changed, some stands of trees may have been felled, or new drainage ditches dug. Map corrections are also used to show any parts of the area which are out of bounds for the event. Whatever the reason, if there are map corrections, make sure you copy them down on to your own map carefully, and accurately, using the correct colour if possible.

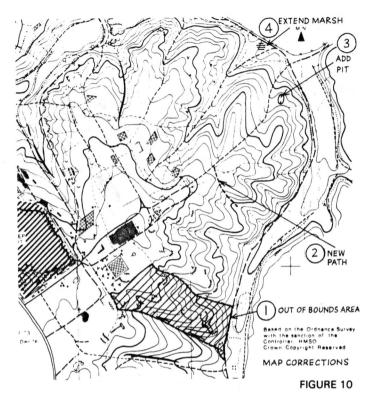

EXTEND MARSH

④

③ ADD PIT

② NEW PATH

① OUT OF BOUNDS AREA

Based on the Ordnance Survey
with the sanction of the
Controller HMSO
Crown Copyright Reserved

MAP CORRECTIONS

FIGURE 10

HAVE YOU FORGOTTEN ANYTHING?

You are now just about ready to go to the start. Before you set off, make one final check that you have everything you need:

Map, in mapcase or transpasealed
Control card
Control description sheet
Compass (if you have one)
Whistle
Pen or pencil
Watch (if you feel you need it)

Then it's off to the start — your first orienteering course is about to begin. The next chapter takes you round the course from the start onwards, and explains some of the basic techniques of orienteering in more detail.

Chapter 6

BASIC TECHNIQUES

AT THE START

This chapter begins where the course itself begins: at the Start. You have selected your course, filled in both parts of your control card, had a look at the map to check the scale, contour interval, and the symbols shown in the legend, and made your way to the start area. The adventure of completing an orienteering course is about to begin. I hope that you will find it enjoyable, stimulating, and sufficiently interesting to make you want to have another go. A little understanding of some of the 'skills of the game' will help.

Please note that some of the illustrations are simplified to make them easier to follow, and are not intended to represent parts of an actual orienteering map.

So here you are at the start. What do you have to do? Well, the start procedure is usually fairly simple. Two or three minutes before your actual start time, you are called up by the pre-start official calling out your time. You hand him or her your control card stub. Each minute after that, a whistle is blown and you move one 'Box' nearer the start line itself (see diagram). You reach the start line one minute before your start time. Here you wait the last nervous seconds until the next whistle — then you're off!

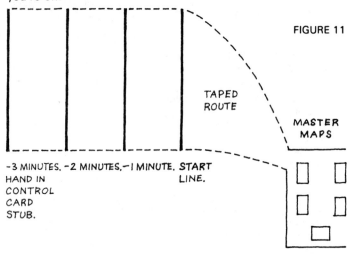

FIGURE 11

TAPED ROUTE

MASTER MAPS

-3 MINUTES. -2 MINUTES. -1 MINUTE. START LINE.
HAND IN CONTROL CARD STUB.

MASTER MAPS

From the start line, a taped route leads a short distance (probably about 200 metres) to the Master Map area. Here, as you would expect, are master copies of each course. You locate your own course (a matter of a few seconds — there will be signs to guide you) and *very carefully* copy down the course on to your own map. Take your time over this, making sure that you get the control circles in exactly the right place. It is worth checking with your control description sheet to see which feature each control is on before drawing the circle on your map. Next number the controls in the correct order round the course, and link them with straight lines. Your position at the Master Maps is shown by a triangle, and the Finish by a double circle. Copy these down too, with equal care.

There should always be enough Master Maps provided to enable all competitors to take their time copying courses down without anyone having to wait to get to a map, but if a queue does develop, don't worry about it — a few extra seconds here are of no significance. Some clubs are now pre-making beginners courses on to the maps before the event, to avoid the possibility of newcomers making an error at Master Maps. If your first event has these pre-marked maps, there will of course be no Master Map procedure — you will simply get your pre-marked map either at registration or at the start, and go off to complete the course from the start.

IMPORTANT NOTE: The Master Maps are for all competitors to use, and on no account must they be taken away.

THE FIRST CONTROL

Having copied your course down, you know where you are (at the point marked by the triangle) and you know where you want to get to (the centre of the circle that indicates control no 1): what you have to decide is the best way to get there. This is called *Route Choice* and is one of the basic skills of orienteering. The first control will probably be very straightforward, but let us consider some of the problems that could arise.

It is important for your confidence to find the first control easily and without problems, and a safe route would always be advised. Stick to the paths if you can, keep checking the map to make sure you know where you are, and keep looking for features along your route to guide you towards the control.

The first thing to decide is the direction in which the first control lies. You can do this in two ways: by taking a rough

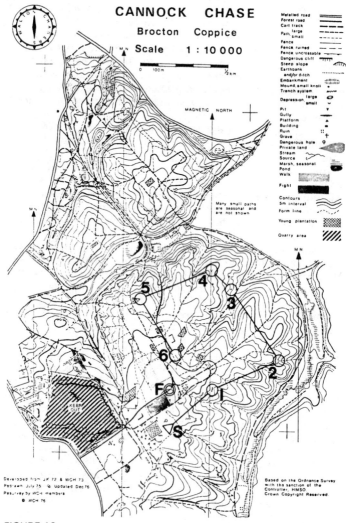

CANNOCK CHASE

Brocton Coppice

Scale 1 : 10 000

FIGURE 12

40

compass bearing, or by orienteering the map. If you have a compass, you will have read the instructions that come with it, and should have practised taking a bearing. This is fully covered in chapter 7. Without a compass, look around for the shape of the land and the direction of the paths and any other features near the start. Now turn your map until the features on the map and the features on the ground coincide. The map is now oriented, or 'set', and you will find it very helpful to try to keep your map set throughout the course. There is more on this technique in Chapter 7.

PATHS OR CROSS-COUNTRY

In British woods, which are extensively worked and almost wholly man-made (unlike the natural forest of Scandinavia) there are extensive path networks, so the orienteer's choice of route is often between a safer, longer path route and a faster, shorter, but riskier 'straight line' route (see illustration).

The latter is more exciting orienteering and will teach, by example, the skills of navigation and fine map-reading which will help you to improve, but I would advise caution in your first few events. Use the paths and 'handrail' features (see below) and get used to knowing exactly where you are on the map all the time, checking off bends, junctions, streams, etc as you pass them. You can lead up to straight line orienteering by cutting corners on path routes where visibility is good and you have a definite feature such as a junction or building to aim for. When you *do* take a direct route, and it comes off, it's a marvellous feeling: but if you try it without really knowing what you're about, you can easily go wrong. So let caution be your watchword to begin with.

HANDRAIL FEATURES

Features shown on orienteering maps are either 'point' (a single object such as a boulder, knoll, or building) or 'linear' (paths, streams, walls). The latter, if clear and reliable, can be used as 'handrails' to help you across the map. At first, you will mainly stick to the paths, these being the safest and clearest features on the ground. With the confidence that comes from successfully completing two or three courses, you will be looking for more direct routes, and 'handrails' will lead you to them. Common handrails in Britain are streams, fences, earth banks and (especially in Northern areas) stone walls. So, if you want to cut a corner and can find a line feature to act as your handrail, you can safely go ahead — but keep checking your position on the map.

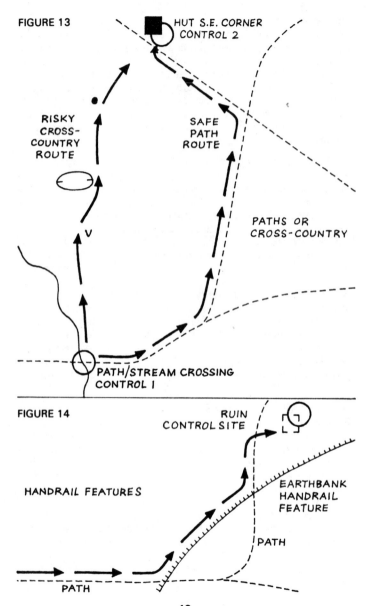

FIGURE 13

HUT S.E. CORNER
CONTROL 2

RISKY
CROSS-
COUNTRY
ROUTE

SAFE
PATH
ROUTE

PATHS OR
CROSS-COUNTRY

PATH/STREAM CROSSING
CONTROL 1

FIGURE 14

RUIN
CONTROL SITE

HANDRAIL FEATURES

EARTHBANK
HANDRAIL
FEATURE

PATH

PATH

42

KEEP READING THE MAP

Orienteering is a navigational sport, and its basic skill is that of map-reading — relating what you read on the map to what you see around you on the ground. Your first few courses will be fairly straightforward and you should be able to complete them without needing to use a compass. This will give you a good start towards the basic skill of reading the map. As we have seen, orienteering maps are very carefully surveyed and drawn, and present a detailed and accurate picture of the terrain. Rely on the map to help you.

From the moment you leave the Master Maps to the moment you punch your card at the last control, *keep reading the map*. I cannot stress the importance of this too much. Don't worry about your speed of travel – it's no use dashing along a path at a great rate if you've no idea what's at the end of it. Keep looking at the map for features on the ground around you, and keep checking off those features as you pass them. This will also help you to develop familiarity with the map symbols and with interpreting them.

If you know where you are on the map, you're not lost — and if you're not lost, you're orienteering correctly and well.

HEIGHT LOSS

Is the next control at the same height as your present position, lower down, or higher up? A look at the contours on the map will tell you. Try to avoid unnecessary height loss. If you can go round a small hill, or skirt a steep-sided valley, rather than climbing up and down, you will save effort and quite probably time as well. There is a point, naturally, at which the detour adds too much extra distance to be worthwhile — but that has to be a matter of individual (sometimes painfully acquired!) judgement.

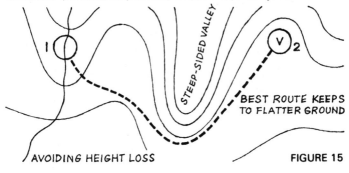

AVOIDING HEIGHT LOSS

STEEP-SIDED VALLEY

BEST ROUTE KEEPS TO FLATTER GROUND

FIGURE 15

ORIENTING THE MAP
Methods of orienting or setting the map are explained above and in the next chapter. It is obviously quicker to locate your position and decide on your next move at path junctions, etc, if your map is correctly set. A left turn on the ground will appear as a right turn on the map if you're heading South but have your map oriented to North.

COMPASS BEARINGS
Methods of taking and following compass bearings are fully covered in Chapter 7.

NEAR THE CONTROL
There are a number of techniques used in the vicinity of the control feature which can be very helpful.

AIMING OFF
The technique of 'aiming off' was first perfected by Sir Francis Chichester in his round-the-world flights in the 1920s. It means that you aim deliberately to one side of the feature you are heading for so that you can turn into it. For example, if the next control is on a stream and you have come cross-country on a bearing towards it, you will be very lucky to hit it 'on the nose'. Therefore you aim left or right and turn in towards the feature when you reach the stream. I always aim left because I tend to drift left off my bearings anyway, but it doesn't matter which side you aim for as long as you know which way to turn when you reach the stream.

Aiming off can obviously only be used with controls which are on line features.

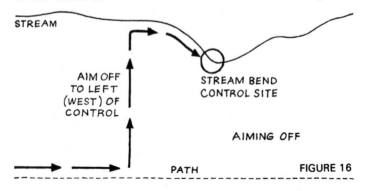

STREAM

AIM OFF
TO LEFT
(WEST) OF
CONTROL

STREAM BEND
CONTROL SITE

AIMING OFF

PATH

FIGURE 16

FIGURE 17

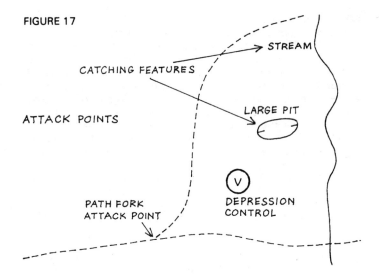

Attack Points

Even with the easiest control, it is useful (and very reassuring) to have a definite feature nearby to aim for, to use for final reference, and from which the control can be 'attacked'. Ideally, this feature should be within 100 metres of the control, and course planners should always bear in mind the need to provide a decent attack point from which the final approach can be made. If you are following a line feature to a control on that feature, and have perhaps used the 'aiming off' technique described above, you may feel an attack point is unnecessary; but something that tells you quite definitely that you are nearing the control and should slow down and look carefully for the marker is always welcome.

If you miss the control from your attack point, look for a *Catching Feature*: some very definite point such as a track or stream junction, wall, large pit, etc. that you can get to easily and that will help you to relocate your position and aim for the control again. It is much better to go on a little way to a definite catching feature and then come back to the control rather than wander around hoping to catch sight of the control marker through the trees. This is a lesson I have not learned (or choose to ignore) after 10 years in the sport, and I know I'm not the only one. If you can learn it early, and stick to it, it will save you a lot of trouble.

What To Do If You Are Lost

'The good orienteer knows where he is, even when he's lost' runs the maxim. This may sound daft, but there's a lot of sense in it. It means he's been checking the features he has passed, and knows, say, that he has crossed two streams, a track, and passed a large knoll on his right. The feature he was aiming for hasn't appeared, he knows (or strongly suspects) he's gone too far, so he tries to relate the features he has passed to the map, to relocate himself. This is the first thing to do if you feel you are lost: try to recall the last place you were certain of your location, and the features you have passed since then, and then try to relate those features to the map.

If this doesn't work, *don't panic*. Don't rush about vaguely looking for something you recognise or can use as a reference: you may find it, but you're more likely to end up more lost than before. You'll almost certainly know which part of the map you're on: look at the map for a catching feature or handrail — something really big — and move towards it, preferably on a simple bearing such as due South (the sun can help you here). If you still can't work out your position, don't be afraid, especially in your first few events, to ask someone where you are. There are usually other orienteers around who will be able to show you your position on the map. Orienteering is basically an individual sport, but our aim is not to put people off by leaving them to get lost for hours, and you will find help is willingly given.

PACING

If you're on a path with a lot of other paths crossing it, and you want to turn right after say 200 metres, it helps not only to know that your turning is the 'third on the right' but that you have actually covered 200 metres, not 150 or 300. The skill of reckoning how far you have travelled while orienteering is called *pacing*.

Pacing is generally based on a unit of 100 metres. At a scale of 1:10,000, 100 metres is represented on the map by 1cm (or 10mm). At 1:15,000 it is 6.6mm, and at 1:20,000 it is 5mm. You can easily measure these map distances, using the scales on the edge of your compass. But how do you know when you have travelled 100 metres?

The only way is by practice. The usual way of pacing is by counting double paces, i.e. each time your left (or right) foot hits the ground, rather than every stride. It's half the counting, and

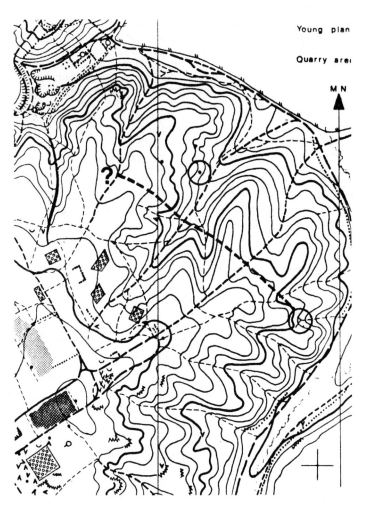

Young plan

Quarry area

M N

You have crossed two major tracks, as you should have done, but have veered left of your correct bearing and hit a third major track. You are unsure of your position, but by orienting the map and seeing that the path bends left and right to run down a steep-sided valley, you will relocate yourself and be able to attack the control again.

FIGURE 18

less mental effort. First you must find yourself a level stretch of ground (preferably grass) and measure out 100 metres as near as you can — perhaps putting a marker of some kind at each end of the stretch. Then cover the 100 metres at your normal orienteering pace, walk, jog, or run, counting the number of double paces. Do this four or five times, noting the reading at the end of each try. Take an average of your readings, and you have your first pacing guide. Running on a flat surface, I take 38 double paces for 100 metres. How many do you take?

If your stride is the same as mine, then you will take about 76 double paces to cover the 200 metres before your turn off the path, as mentioned above. Counting up to 76 while running and trying to read a map may sound a bit difficult, and at first it undoubtedly is, but it is worth trying to acquire the basic skill of pacing. In British woods, you will not infrequently be faced with a path run of several hundred metres, and if you can rely on your pacing to tell you when you've covered the required distance, you can turn the other half of your brain to looking at the next two or three navigational problems, or the approach to the control after you have turned off the path.

Pacing can, of course, be used over any terrain, not just on paths. But you will find your paces per 100 metres vary according to the roughness of the ground and the slope, if there is one. It is up to each orienteer to work out his or own pacing scales, but I hope these notes will have given you an idea of how to start.

Pacing is undoubtedly useful, very useful, and could be vital in locating your position. But, like compass work, it is a supplementary to the basic orienteering skill of reading the map and relating the map to the ground. Many orienteers get by quite happily without pacing at all, so if it seems an unnecessary complication, don't worry about it until your other basic techniques are well developed.

Chapter 7

USING THE COMPASS

After the map, the compass is the orienteer's best friend. It is used for taking a bearing; travelling on a bearing; setting the map; and is a vital aid in the fine navigation of reaching the control from your chosen attack point.

A word of warning will not be out of place: the modern orienteering compass is a splendid precision instrument, robust in construction and simple to use once you get the hang of it. It is *not* a magic guide to completing orienteering courses. Compass work is a valuable skill and you will find many uses for it outside orienteering, but it is only one of the many techniques used by the good orienteer.

THE ORIENTEERING COMPASS

The protractor-type compass was developed for orienteering in Sweden by the Kjellstrom brothers about 40 years ago, and their company, Silva, make many of the compasses used by orienteers all over the world. There are other makes, notably the Finnish Suunto, but all orienteering compasses are of basically similar construction, as shown in the diagram.

The orienteering compass has two main components, that in other types of compass are separate. The *baseplate* (or protractor) is made of strong transparent plastic and normally has various scales along its edges that measure map distance in inches and millimetres. A version recently developed especially for orienteering has detachable scales at the front edge only. They can be changed to conform to the scale of the map in use on the day.

The *housing* is mounted on the base plate but can be freely rotated. On the baseplate is a *direction-of-travel arrow;* other direction lines are engraved on the base plate parallel to it, and of course the longer edges of the compass are frequently used when taking bearings from a map, as explained later.

The housing contains a *North arrow* etched into the bottom surface. You will see several other parallel lines on the housing, also known as North§South lines.

The *magnetic needle* is freely mounted in the compass housing, which is filled with a special oil to slow down or 'dampen' the needle's movement. These needles are much more stable than those in undamped compasses and rapid travel on an accurate bearing is possible when using a Silva-type compass.

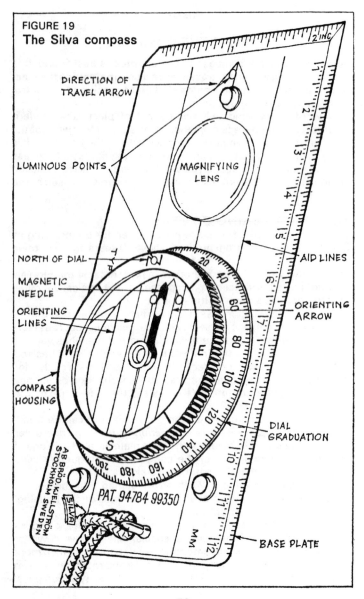

FIGURE 19
The Silva compass

DIRECTION OF TRAVEL ARROW

LUMINOUS POINTS

MAGNIFYING LENS

NORTH OF DIAL

MAGNETIC NEEDLE

ORIENTING LINES

AID LINES

ORIENTING ARROW

COMPASS HOUSING

DIAL GRADUATION

AB BRÖD. KJELLSTRÖM STOCKHOLM SWEDEN

SILVA

PAT. 94784 99350

MM

BASE PLATE

The magnetic needle has one end painted red and one end white. The red end always points to magnetic north – unless you happen to be near to an iron object. As orienteering maps are always aligned to magnetic north and not the grid north used on Ordnance Survey maps, the north indicated by your compass needle corresponds to the north lines drawn on your map.

USING THE COMPASS
Let's now take a look at the main ways in which the orienteer uses the compass.

TAKING A BEARING
This is the basic compass skill and you should practice it until you can just about do it with your eyes closed. Any map will serve 'or practice; if you have a street map or OS map of your area, take :he compass with you on a walk and take bearings each time you change direction. Or you can use the example maps used in this book. The technique of taking a bearing is very simple, and divides into three steps.

1: Set your direction. Place a long side of the compass between your present location and your destination (start and control 1 on the map). Be careful to ensure that the direction-of-travel arrow on the baseplate in pointing *towards* your destination (i.e. the front edge of the compass is by control 1).

2: Set the North/South lines. Keep the compass base held firmly on the map so that neither moves and turn the housing round until the N/S lines are exactly parallel to the North lines on the map. The North arrow *(not the magnetic needle)* on the housing must be pointing to North on the map.

3: Set yourself. Take the compass from the map and hold it flat in your hand in front of your stomach, with the direction-of-travel arrow (front edge of the compass) pointing away from you. Now *turn yourself around* until the red (North) end of the magnetic needle is aligned exactly with the North/South lines on the housing (not the lines on the base). Make absolutely sure that the *red* end of the floating needle is over the *North* mark on the housing – otherwise you will go in exactly the wrong direction!

You are now facing in the direction you wish to travel and can proceed on your bearing – more of that in a moment. What have we just done? In three simple steps, we located the line of direction to travel between the start and control 1; transferred to the compass the angle between the North lines on the map and our desired direction of travel; and finally transferred this angle to the terrain

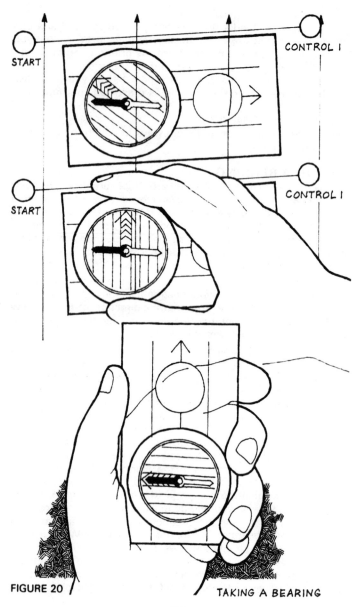

START

CONTROL I

START

CONTROL I

FIGURE 20

TAKING A BEARING

by making the North arrow on the compass point to North on the housing.

Simple enough? If anything is not clear, go back to the beginning of this section and read through it again, carrying out the three steps with your compass as you do so. Very soon you will be taking bearings automatically; once learned, this technique is never forgotten.

TRAVELLING ON A BEARING

Now that you can take a bearing, the next step is to travel on that bearing. There are four steps here. As you become more experienced and quicker at compass work, they merge into one operation, but to begin with, let's consider them separately.

1: Holding the compass flat in front of you, double check to be sure that the magnetic needle still covers the North arrow.

2: Now take a sighting. Look down at the compass, then sight along the direction of travel arrow, then look up, maintaining the line of sight. Pick a landmark at a reasonable distance — say 100 metres away (roughly the length of a football pitch, if it helps). It can be a large tree, a boulder, a hump in the ground — anything that stands out.

3: Take the easiest route to your landmark, avoiding dense undergrowth and other obstacles if there are any. You don't need to use the compass on the way.

4: When you reach the landmark, repeat the sighting procedure (step 2) and so on until you reach your destination. Keep the distances between your landmarks fairly short to begin with to reduce the risk of error.

Using this simple procedure, you can travel on a bearing for as far as you need. Let me repeat again keep in touch with the map all the time, so that you know where you are and what your next significant map feature is.

SETTING THE MAP

You will find it easier to follow the map on the ground if map and terrain are 'set' or orientated so that the features on the ground line up with those drawn on the map. It's easy to set your map. First, put the compass on the map with the needle (don't worry about the way it's pointing) close to a magnetic north line. Then, turn compass and map together until the needle is parallel to the north lines on the map, and the red end of the needle is pointing to the north edge of the map. The map is now set — take the

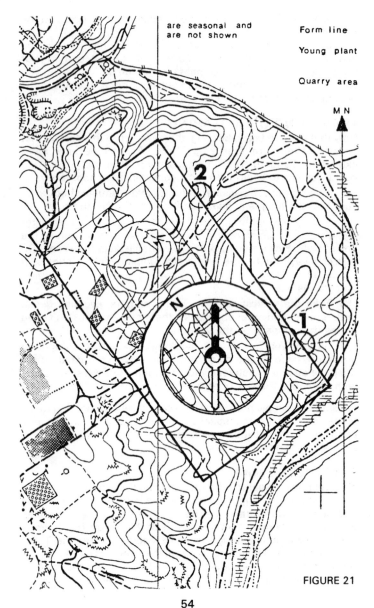

are seasonal and
are not shown

Form line

Young plant

Quarry area

M N

N

2

1

FIGURE 21

54

compass away without moving the map, and when you compare the map with the terrain around you, you should find for example that the paths run away from you in the same direction as they do on the map.

Suddenly it all starts to make sense! Try to keep your map set as much as you can. It's worth taking time in your first few events to practice this vital skill each time you come to a path junction or a major feature such as a stream.

You can also practice map setting using Ordnance Survey or street maps. It soon enough becomes a habit. Experienced orienteers keep their maps set all the time.

RUNNING ON THE NEEDLE

This is a somewhat more advanced technique, but as a logical progression from keeping the map set, it is as well to mention it here. All it means is that, instead of taking the compass away from the map when you have it set, you keep the compass on the map as you move along. By keeping the north end of the needle lined up with the north edge of the map, along the grid lines, you ensure that you are travelling in the right direction. Place one long edge of the compass along your line of travel, and then set the map as before.

These are the basic compass skills. Practice them often until you are confident in their use. Remember two things — (a) keep reading the map — don't rely entirely on the compass; (b) the compass is very rarely wrong. If map and compass don't seem to relate, look at the map, and the terrain, again. It's almost certainly you that's wrong.

Chapter 8

TYPES OF ORIENTEERING

CROSS-COUNTRY ORIENTEERING

The 'cross-country' event is the basic and most often practised type of orienteering. The name is slightly misleading in that the course may not be a line across country but, due to the shape of the area being used, the facilities available. or simply the course planner's fancy, may be circular, triangular, or eccentric in shape.

The basic concept is, however, always the same. The event starts from A (The Start) and proceeds via B, C, D, etc (the Controls) to X (the Finish). All controls must be visited in set order, as shown on the control description sheet and the master maps.

If there is no indication on event details of the type of orienteering, you can safely assume that it is a cross-country event.

SCORE EVENTS

In a cross-country event, the winner of each course or class is the person completing the course, visiting all the controls in the correct order, in the shortest time. Score events work differently. A large number of controls (often 20 or 25) are put out and competitors have to visit as many as they can, in any order, within a defined time limit (usually one hour). Each control is given a points value according to its distance from the start and difficulty, and the winner is the person with the most points. If more than one competitor visits all the controls within the time allowed, the fastest is the winner.

Score events are relatively simple to organise as there are no 'courses' to plan, and are great fun to take part in. The route-finding problems can be tricky: you normally have to decide at the start (which is commonly also the finish) which way round you're going to go and how far you can get before you have to think of turning back. Penalties are given for being late, so a watch is necessary. Don't forget to synchronise your watch with the official start time before you set off.

Score events are sometimes arranged with a 'mass start' when all competitors leave at once. This has the advantage for the organisers that the whole thing is over in an hour or so and they can join the competitors in the pub or clubhouse afterwards. Mass start score events are arranged for such times as New Year's Day, to give everyone a little healthy exercise and clear the head from the night before. It is hilarious to watch people dashing off in all directions as the start whistle is blown!

The Scots organise Score Championships in February each year, but the practice has not yet spread south of the border.

COME-AND-TRY-IT (CATI) EVENTS

As might be gathered from the name, CATI events are aimed at beginners. They are normally cross-country type events with very short, easy courses in simple terrain such as parks or commons close to large centres of population (e.g. Wimbledon Common in London or Braid Hills in Edinburgh). Usually, only two courses are offered — short and very short — and experienced orienteers are on hand to give advice and instruction. The courses are deliberately made very easy to complete, to give the novice orienteer confidence. Those completing the shortest course without any problem are usually offered the chance to try a longer one at no extra charge.

CATI events may be advertised as 'Introductory' or 'Beginners' events. They are a very good way to start orienteering as it is almost impossible *not* to complete the courses successfully and, with your confidence thus boosted and having enjoyed your first event, you will be keen to come back for more.

MAP MEMORY EVENTS

In map memory events, competitors are shown the position of the controls at the start but not allowed to copy them down — or even to take a map. They then have to set off into the unknown trying to memorise the position of the controls and the routes between them. To avoid undue brain damage, these events often operate one control at a time — at the start you are shown only the position of the first control. Assuming you reach it, another portion of map will show you the way to no 2, and so on round the course until the dazed orienteer staggers into the finish. Cruel organisers may put out 'dummy' controls to tempt the unwary.

Map memory events are obviously intended basically as training exercises for experience orienteers. They are certainly not suitable for beginners. They do have a certain fascination and there is a considerable sense of achievement (and relief) in finishing a map memory course.

LINE EVENTS

Depending on the terrain, line events can be excellent training for those fairly new to orienteering (i.e. not absolute beginners).

Instead of having a list of controls and choosing your route between them, the organiser chooses the route and you copy this onto your map as a continuous line. You then set off to follow the line precisely on the ground. At irregular distances along the line you will find control markers. When you reach a marker, you must note its position on your map. You are usually not told before you start how many controls there are. When you get back to the finish, you check with a 'master map' to see if you found all the controls.

Line events can help to teach you to follow the map very closely, and to relate the map to the ground. Hopefully the organiser will not be too cruel — I fancy Puck, in Shakespeare's A Midsummer Night's Dream, had been doing a line event when he spoke of travelling 'thorough bush, thorough briar'.

NIGHT EVENTS

The main difference with night events is that they take place after dark! It is therefore necessary for competitors to carry some form of torch or headlamp in order to see where they are going and to read the map.

Night events are popular in Scandinavia, where they are held throughout the summer, starting at midnight or even later. They have not caught on so much in Britain and are normally a winter activity here, with starts in the early evening. They are a very good way of using open or parkland areas which would be simple to navigate across by day but can provide really first-class orienteering at night. Enclosed areas of moorland or large city parks are both ideal for night orienteering.

Courses in night events are usually about one third shorter than their daylight equivalents. Night events are not suitable for inexperienced orienteers but they have a charm all their own and I strongly recommend anyone to try one once you have become proficient by day. The twinkling, moving lights from competitors' torches at a night event make a beautiful and slightly eerie sight. A light headlamp is often used to avoid the need for a third hand to hold the torch (the other two being occupied with map and compass).

RELAYS

Having stressed that orienteering is an individual sport, we are now going to talk about team events! The relay is a very exciting form of orienteering, however, and is probably the only time orienteering becomes a spectator sport. Here's how it works.

Teams are normally of 3 runners, each having to complete a cross-country course in the normal way. First leg runners are set off in a mass start and their team-mates then wait anxiously for any sign of them returning to the start/finish area (always the same place). When a first leg runner comes back, he hands over to the second runner in the team, usually by touch, and off goes number two to run his course. He comes back and sets off number three. When the third runner returns, the team has finished. In this type of orienteering, as in no other, the first one back on the third leg is the winner (provided all three have completed their courses correctly).

Relays are great fun to take part in, and exciting to watch. For the competitor, they introduce a whole new pressure; he knows that the fellow ahead of him in the forest is also just ahead of him in the race, and to pass him is to gain a place. Relays are often won or lost by very small errors. I think the 1976 World Championships Relays in Scotland was the most exciting orienteering event I have ever attended, and even if you are not taking part it can be well worth while going to a relay even just to watch.

SKI ORIENTEERING

Ski-O could be called a competitive form of the increasingly popular sport of cross-country, or langlauf, ski-ing. It is very popular in Scandinavia as a way of keeping fit in the long winter, and attempts are being made to get it going in Britain — the obvious problem being the lack of lasting snow cover in most areas.

Ski-O courses are much longer than 'foot-O' and have fewer controls: a typical men's Ski-O course would be 20-25km with 4 or 5 controls. The competitor on skis naturally travels faster than the foot orienteer.

If you have some experience of ski-ing, ski-O could be an interesting variation for you to try.

Chapter 9

THE STRUCTURE OF THE SPORT

BRITISH ORIENTEERING FEDERATION

As has been mentioned, the sport of orienteering in Britain is administered by the British Orienteering Federation. The Federation's central office in Derbyshire looks after membership and administration, and the Professional Officer, working from there, directs the development and promotion of the sport.

For practical reasons, events are staged not by the Federation but by its twelve autonomous regional associations and by the clubs belonging to them.

The Regional Associations

The 12 regional bodies and the areas they cover are:—

Scottish Orienteering Association	—the whole of Scotland
Northern Ireland OA	—the whole of N. Ireland
North Western OA	—Cumbria, Lancashire, Cheshire, Greater Manchester
North Eastern OA	—Northumberland, Durham, Cleveland, a small part of North Yorkshire
Yorkshire and Humberside OA	—Yorkshire, North and South Humberside
Welsh OA	—all of Wales
West Midlands OA	—Staffordshire, Hereford and Worcester, County of West Midlands, Warwickshire
East Midlands OA	—Derbyshire, Leicestershire, Northamptonshire, Lincolnshire
East Anglian OA	—Norfolk, Suffolk, Cambridgeshire, Bedfordshire, Eastern Essex
South Eastern OA	—West Essex, Hertfordshire, Greater London, Kent, Surrey, Sussex
South Central OA	—Oxon, Buckinghamshire, Hampshire, Berkshire
South West OA	—Gloucestershire, Avon, Somerset, Dorset, Devon, Cornwall

You will be able to tell from this list which region you live in. The address of the regional secretary and of club secretaries for your region can be obtained from BOF National Office.

CLUBS AND GROUPS

Each region has a number of clubs affiliated to it. Most orienteering events are staged by clubs, working to a fixture list co-ordinated a year or more ahead by the regional fixtures secretary. Large events such as championships are staged by regions, combining the manpower and expertise of several clubs to cope with the large numbers of competitors at these events.

There are now over 100 orienteering clubs in Britain, so there is almost bound to be one not far from you. It's a good idea to join a club, even if you're only an occasional orienteer, as your club will keep you supplied with information on future events, club nights, socials and so on. You will also be able to talk orienteering with more experienced orienteers (and other beginners — swopping tales of triumph or disaster!) and learn more about the techniques of the sport by joining a club.

HOW TO JOIN

There are three 'tiers' of membership in orienteering, and several grades within each tier. You can join as an individual, senior or junior (under 19), as a family, or as a group. This last cetegory allows schools, scouts, youth clubs and the like to affiliate to a region of BOF and thus receive literature and information without all their members having to join individually. Family membership allows mother, father, and one or two children under 19 to join for one fee (about 1½ times the senior individual fee).

Club membership is very inexpensive but gives correspondingly little in return. Club members receive club newsletters and fixture lists, compete only in local events, and can vote only at club annual general meetings.

Associate membership is the middle tier. Associate members receive club and regional newsletters, can compete in all events up to regional championship level, and can vote at regional AGM's.

Full membership brings club and regional newsletters and the sport's excellent national magazine **The Orienteer** which is published bi-monthly. Full members are free to compete in all events including the national championships, and can vote at the Federations's AGM, which is traditionally held on the evening before the national championships in May or June each year.

Details of current membership fees can be obtained from club or regional secretaries or from BOF national office. As an example, in 1978 a senior individual would pay about 50 pence for club membership for one year, £1.50-£2 for associate membership, and about £5 for full membership. Junior fees are roughly half the senior equivalent, and family members pay a single fee of about 1½ times the senior individual fee.

THE SEASON IN BRITAIN

The orienteering season in Britain runs roughly from September to June, with most of the major events and championships held between March and May. There is a shut-down in the summer months for the simple reason that, in most areas, the undergrowth — particularly brambles and bracken — gets too high and dense in forests for orienteering to be a pleasurable activity.

The prime period for orienteering, to my mind, is in the spring when the young leaves are just appearing on the deciduous trees, visibility is still good, and there is little or no undergrowth to check your progress. To run in mature woods on a fine day in late spring or early summer is simply a delight.

REGIONAL AND NATIONAL CHAMPIONSHIPS

There are four regional championships held annually — the Scottish, Northern, Midland, and Southern. The three English championships are organised on a rota basis by different regions in turn, the allocation being:

Northern — North West, North East, Yorkshire & Humberside
Midlands — Wales, West Midlands, East Midlands, East Anglia
Southern — South West, South Central, South East

At the time of writing, the Midlands Championships are normally held in late February or early March, the Southern in April, the Scottish in May, and the Northern in September.

Any *full* member of BOF may compete in *any* regional championships, and indeed one of the great pleasures of orienteering for me is travelling to different regions to run over different types of terrain. Within a comparatively short period, one can sample the intricate contour detail of Cannock Chase, the rough heather and steep-sided valleys of North Yorkshire, and the rolling deciduous woods of Surrey — all posing different navigational and physical problems.

At present there are no 'qualifying standards' applied for full members, and I very much hope it stays that way. It does mean that championships have entries of up to 2000 competitors, but the level of organisational ability in all regions is now well able to cope with such numbers.

Associate members may compete only in their own regional championships. You can run in the Midlands Championships — but not the Northern — if you live in Leicester or North Wales. If you live in Yorkshire or Cumbria the reverse applies.

Club members are not eligible to run in Championships.

The British Championships are held in late May or early June and are organised by different region each year. This event is the climax of the season, and is of considerable sophistication, with a public address system, full prizegiving by a dignitary (we were honoured to welcome Mr Denis Howell, the Minister for Sport, to the 1977 championships) and other trimmings not found at local events. One thing the organisers cannot control, unfortunately, is the weather, and I have run in 'Nationals' in everything from a heatwave to cold rain and mist. All full BOF members, individual or family, but not associate members, may enter the national championships.

There is also a national relay championships, held in April or May, and there are plans for inaugurating a national night championships. The other major event in the British orienteering calendar is the Jan Kjellström Trophy meeting, held over the Easter weekend in a different region each year. This is an international multi-day event that draws hundreds of entries from abroad. It has a unique atmosphere and for many orienteers, 'JK' is one of the highlights of the year.

ORIENTEERING ABROAD

The summer shut-down in Britain coincides very conveniently with the dates of the major events in Europe, where the undergrowth is much less of a problem. There are many three- or five-day events, notable in Sweden, Norway, and Switzerland, round which a splendid holiday can be arranged. Orienteering abroad is tremendously enjoyable — even if you don't do very well! — and I thoroughly recommend it. But don't go until you've had a couple of years experience of the sport and feel ready to tackle foreign maps and terrain.

The recent introduction of pictorial description sheets for international events means that lack of understanding of the native language is no longer a problem.

THE WORLD CHAMPIONSHIPS

Orienteering is an Olympic sport — that is, it is recognised by the International Olympic Committee, although it does not at present feature in the programme for the Olympic Games. The sport's topmost event is the World Championships (WOC) which is staged by a different member-nation of the International Orienteering Federation every two years. The event is moving from the even-numbered to the odd-numbered years in 1979 to avoid clashes with the Olympics.

Britain had the honour of the staging WOC in 1976, and the championship races were run in Darnaway and Culbin Forests, in Scotland, with Aviemore as the event centre. It was generally agreed to have been the best WOC yet staged — a considerable distinction in view of our short life as an orienteering nation. The only shortcoming was that we were not able to provide a British world champion! As usual, most of the top awards went to Scandinavia. The men's champion was Egil Johansen from Norway and the women's Liisa Veijalainen from Finland. Sweden won both men's and women's relays, with the British men 6th, their best placing so far.

As there are 21 nations in IOF, it is likely to be some while before Britain is asked to stage WOC again. The 1979 event is in Finland, 1981 in Switzerland, and 1983 in France.